Headaches

Dr. Alvin Silverstein,

Virginia Silverstein, and

Laura Silverstein Nunn

My Health

Franklin Watts

A Division of Scholastic Inc.

New York • Toronto • London • Auckland • Sydney

Mexico City • New Delhi • Hong Kong

Danbury, Connecticut

Photographs ©: Craig D. Wood: 35; Jim Whitmer: 12, 16; Nance S. Trueworthy: 17, 30; Photo Researchers, NY: 23, 24 (John Bavosi/SPL), 28 (CNRI/SPL), 37 (Ken Lax), 9 (Quest/SPL), 18 (Blair Seitz), 10 (Paul Singh-Roy/SS), 33 (Hattie Young/SPL); PhotoEdit: 7, 11 (Myrleen Ferguson Cate), 32 (Tom McCarthy), 14 (David Young-Wolff); Stock Boston: 38 (Bob Daemmrich), 15 (Lawrence Migdale), 8 (Jeffrey Myers); The Image Works/Ogust: 26; Visuals Unlimited: 4, 21 (Nancy P. Alexander), 31 (R. Calentine), 22 (Jeff Greenberg).

Cartoons by Rick Stromoski

Library of Congress Cataloging-in-Publication Data

Silverstein, Alvin.
    Headaches / by Alvin Silverstein, Virginia Silverstein, and Laura Silverstein Nunn.
        p. cm.—(My Health)
    Includes bibliographical references and index.
    ISBN 0-531-11872-X (lib. bdg.)   0-531-16561-2 (pbk.)
    1. Headache—Juvenile literature. [1. Headache.] I. Silverstein, Virginia B.
    II. Nunn, Laura Silverstein III. Title IV. Series
    RC392.S528   2001
 616.8'491—dc21   00-051355

Contents

Oh, My Aching Head!

What a busy day at school! You survive a pop quiz and an exhausting gym class, but then you almost miss the bus. When you get home, you plop down in your favorite chair, lean back, and moan, "Oh, my head hurts!" You have a headache.

A headache is a sign that something is wrong in your body. Many things can cause headaches—a tough day at school, certain foods,

Did You Know...

Most people get a headache every once in a while. As many as 75 percent of children have had some bad headaches by the time they are 15 years old.

◀ **Do you ever feel like this?**

or the flashing special effects on a TV show. You can even get a headache when you're hungry, or when you don't get enough sleep. Many common illnesses can also cause headaches.

Not all headaches are the same. Most are just an annoying dull ache that makes it hard to think. But

some are *really* bad. They make you feel like your head is going to explode. The pain may be constant, or it may throb—like a heartbeat.

Headaches can be a real pain, but most are not serious. Sometimes, though, headaches hurt so much or happen so often that you need to see a doctor. A doctor can help you find out what is causing the headaches. Once you know what the problem is, you can find ways to treat the headaches or get rid of them completely.

Would you like to learn more about headaches? Read on to find out what causes headaches and what you should do when you get one.

Most people get a head-ache once in a while.

7

What Is a Headache?

Headaches are among the most common health problems in the United States. Millions of adults and kids suffer from headaches. Even young children quickly learn to identify the pain of a hurting head.

Lots of adults get headaches when they are at work.

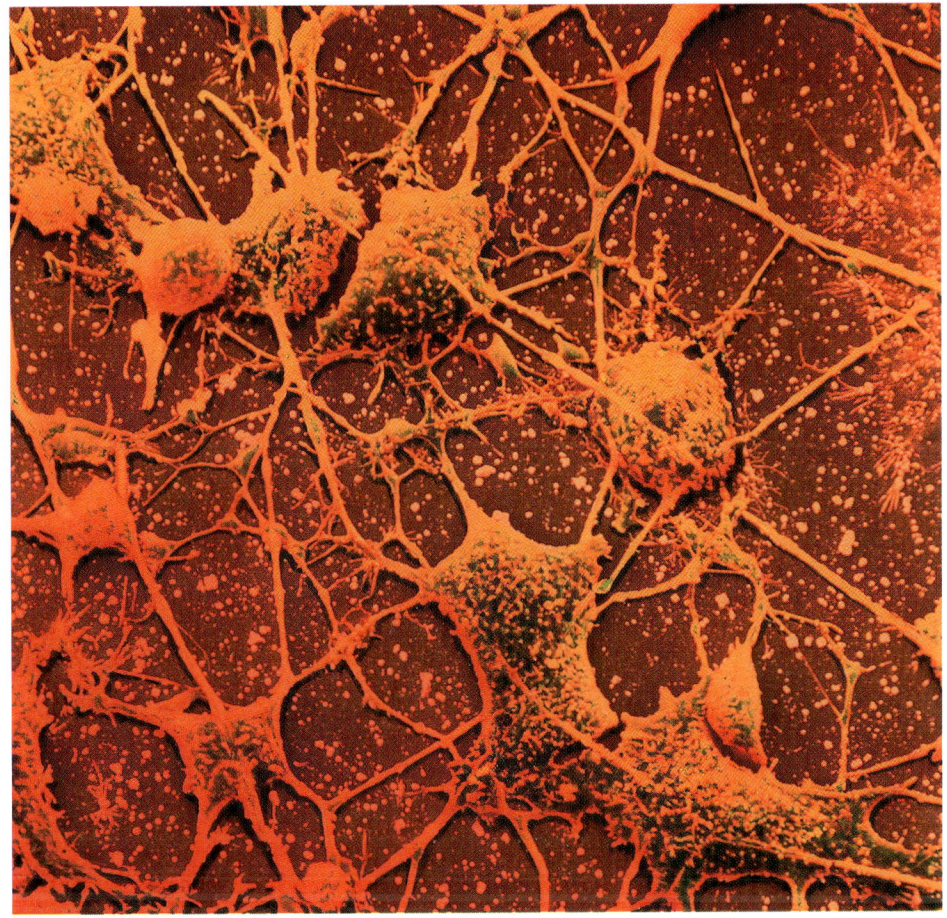

Nerve cells, such as the ones shown here, carry messages to the brain, where they are turned into something we can understand— like pain!

When you have a headache, the pain seems to be coming from inside your head. At first you might think your brain is hurt, but that isn't really true. Your brain is the control center for all your thoughts, feelings, and body movements. Information about the world travels from your eyes, ears, nose, mouth, and skin to your brain. These messages are carried by **nerves**.

When you get hurt, nerves carry pain messages to your brain. But your brain does not have nerve endings that can sense pain. If your brain were damaged, you wouldn't feel any pain. In fact, a doctor can operate on a person's brain while he or she is awake!

So what is it that's hurting when you have a headache? Most of the time, it's the nerves, **blood vessels**, or muscles in your **scalp** or neck. Blood

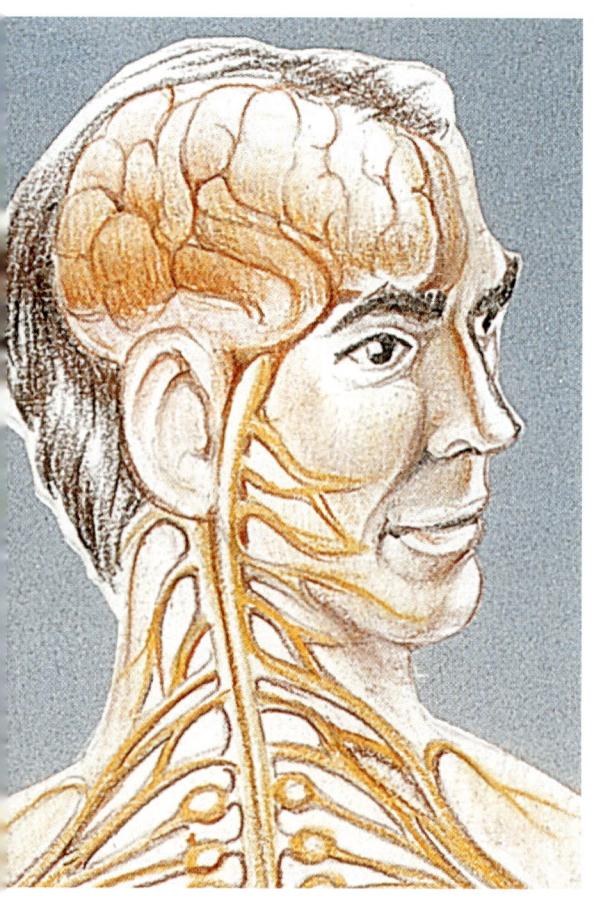

vessels in and around your brain can hurt too. They may swell up and put pressure on nearby nerves. Nerves in your face, mouth, or throat may also be responsible. When any of these nerves send pain messages to your brain, you get a headache.

Most people get headaches every once in a while. Some people get headaches more often. They may get a headache several times a week—or even every day. A headache may last for a few minutes, a few hours, or a few days.

You may get a headache when the blood vessels in your head or neck swell up and press on nearby nerves, sending pain messages to the brain.

Headache pain may be rather mild or really annoying. A bad headache can make you want to just curl up and go to sleep, but sometimes headaches hurt so much that you can't sleep.

There are two main kinds of headaches—**tension-type headaches** and **migraine headaches**. When you have a tension-type headache, you feel a dull pain that just won't let up. It feels like something is pressing on your head. The pain may be in the front or back of your head or on both sides. Sometimes a tension-type headache feels like a tight band around your head.

Homework has really stressed this boy out. Now he feels headache pain in the back of his head.

A migraine is a different kind of headache. The pain is sharp and throbbing, and it is usually in just one area. The name *migraine* comes from a Greek word meaning "half a head" because migraine pain often occurs on just one side of the head. But some

migraines make both sides of your head hurt, or the pain may spread from one side to the other. You may also be unusually sensitive to bright light, loud noises, or strong smells.

A migraine is sometimes called a "sick headache" because it can make you feel dizzy or sick to your stomach. You may even throw up.

Some headaches are a combination of both migraine and tension-type headaches. You may start out with a migraine. Then, if the pain makes you tighten muscles in your head and neck, you may end up with tension-type headache too. In some situations, a tension-type headache may also bring on a migraine.

Tension-type headaches are more common than migraines. About 90 percent of the people who complain about headaches have tension-type headaches.

What Causes Headaches?

Believe it or not, a headache is actually meant to help you, not hurt you. A headache is your body's way of telling you that something is wrong.

Many different things can trigger a headache. A change in your everyday activities—such as getting too much or too little sleep—can bring on a

It looks like somebody didn't get enough sleep.

14

headache. So can skipping a meal or eating much later than usual. A very bumpy bus ride can make your head hurt too.

You may get a headache when you feel sad, angry, worried or upset. When you worry about a test at school or troubles at home, your head may start to hurt. You may also develop a headache if you are really upset after a fight with a good friend.

Some people get headaches from the smell of smoke, perfume, a new carpet, or fumes from paint or gasoline. The flickering glare of a TV or computer monitor can also trigger a headache. Some people get headaches when they eat chocolate, cheese, yogurt, citrus fruits, bananas, bacon, bologna, or hot dogs. **Caffeine** can trigger headaches too. So can food additives, such as NutraSweet and monosodium glutamate (MSG).

Wearing a mask can help to protect you from breathing in harmful paint fumes.

15

Brain Freeze

Did you ever get a headache after eating ice cream? People often call this a "brain freeze." When ice cream touches the roof of your mouth, the cold temperature sets off a nerve at the back of your throat, and that causes a headache. Ice pops, slushy frozen drinks, or even cold soda, milk, or juice can also give you a brain freeze.

Luckily, this kind of headache usually goes away in just a few minutes. If you start to feel a brain freeze coming on, try holding your tongue against the roof of your mouth. This will warm the area and may help you avoid the headache.

Oh no! Brain freeze!

Headaches that develop after a head injury may be a sign of serious trouble. Normally, your skull protects your brain, but when you hit your head, your brain may crash against your skull. If blood vessels are damaged, they will bleed and swell, causing a painful headache. If you get a headache after falling off your bike or tripping down the stairs, see a doctor right away.

In rare cases, headaches may be caused by a brain **tumor**. When a tumor grows inside the brain, it pushes normal brain tissues aside and presses against them. Because most brain tissues do not sense pain, the person usually doesn't feel any pain until the tumor is fairly large. As the tumor continues to grow, the headaches gradually get worse and happen more often. If doctors catch a brain tumor early, they may be able to remove it.

This boy should have been wearing a helmet. If he develops headaches, it could be a sign of brain damage.

All About Headaches

When you are watching an interesting TV show or playing an exciting video game, you may not realize that you are sitting in an uncomfortable position. But when the show or game is over, your body aches and your head hurts. You have a full-blown tension-type headache.

Tension-type headaches occur when muscles in your face, neck, or scalp tense up, or tighten, for long periods of time. Your muscles may tighten when you are worried about something. Studying hard for a test or watching TV too long can also make your head and neck muscles tighten.

Sitting in an uncomfortable position can give you a headache, but you may not notice the problem until it is too late.

If you have a tension-type headache, you may find it hard to think or pay attention. But this type of headache is not usually serious enough to keep you from doing things—even though you may feel miserable doing them.

Migraines are a different story. A migraine can make you feel so tired that you just want to lie down. Migraines may be so painful that you cannot take part in everyday activities. You may not even want to get up and walk around.

You are more likely to get migraines if one of your parents, grandparents, aunts, uncles, or some other family member gets them. If one of your parents gets migraines, there's a 50 percent chance that you will get them. If both of your parents get migraines, you have a 75 percent chance of getting them.

There are two main kinds of migraine headaches—migraines with **aura** and migraines without aura. A person who has a migraine with aura may be able to

Did You Know...

Carrying around a heavy bookbag can give you a headache, especially when you carry it over one shoulder. That's because you raise your shoulder against the weight of the bag and tighten the muscles of your shoulder and neck.

sense when a headache is coming on. During a period called the **prodrome**, the person may feel sad, crabby, or restless. Some people are forgetful. Others lose their appetite, yawn a lot, or become sensitive to lights, sounds, and smells.

Shortly before the headache starts, a person having a migraine with aura may experience some really weird things. Some people start to see bright flashing lights and quivering, zigzagging lines. During this period, which doctors call the aura, people may also feel numbness and tingling—especially in their lips or hands. If they try to read, it may seem like words are missing from some parts of the page. People may even have trouble talking or experience muscle weakness.

Did You Know...

The British writer Lewis Carroll often suffered from migraines. His auras were quite unusual. Instead of flashing zigzags or numbness, he had **hallucinations**. He saw and heard things that weren't there! Lewis based many of the unusual incidents in his famous book *Alice's Adventures in Wonderland* on his strange hallucinations.

Migraine pain usually begins 10 to 30 minutes after the aura starts. During the headache, any kind of movement makes migraine pain worse. After the pain stops, the person may feel "wiped out."

Only about 10 to 20 percent of people who get migraines experience an aura. The rest have migraines without aura. They have no obvious warning signs, but the headache pain is just as bad.

This girl feels something coming on. It could be early signs of a migraine.

Migraines
may make
you want to
crawl into
bed and hide
from the
world.

Medical experts say that migraines result from changes in the level of certain chemicals in the brain, especially a substance called **serotonin**. Serotonin helps nerves carry messages from one part of the brain to another. This chemical controls your mood, how well you sleep, and the widening or narrowing of your blood vessels.

A migraine may begin when a person is exposed to bright flashing lights, feels worried or upset, or eats certain foods. These things are triggers. They cause the amount of serotonin in the person's brain to increase. Then blood vessels become narrow, or **constrict**.

The brain normally receives a rich supply of blood. The blood is full of oxygen and sugar to power the body's activities. When blood vessels constrict, important parts of the brain do not get enough blood. Then a person may see flashing lights or feel dizzy or numb.

A migraine does not stop there. Serotonin leaks out of blood vessels into surrounding tissues, lowering the amount of serotonin in the brain. The lack of serotonin makes it easier for other sense messages to get through. That is probably why people with migraines are often very sensitive to light, noise, and smells. The lack of serotonin also causes blood vessels in the head to swell and widen, or **dilate**. The

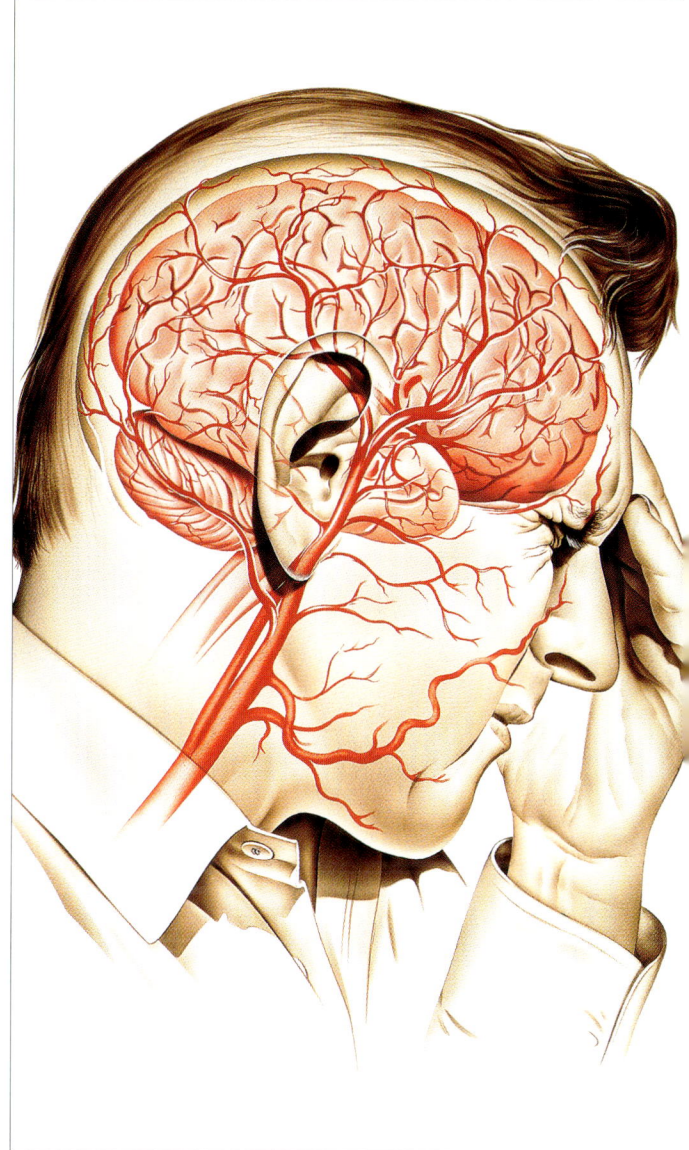

During a migraine, an increase of serotonin in the brain causes blood vessels to swell up.

swollen blood vessels press on nearby nerves, and the painful part of the headache begins.

Why does migraine pain throb? It seems almost like a heartbeat. Actually, it is a reflection of the heart's beating. Your heart is a pump. The strong muscles in its walls contract in a steady rhythm, pushing blood into a network of **arteries** that carry it to every part of your body. After each heartbeat—as a surge of blood gushes through the arteries—muscles in the walls of your arteries contract too. This helps keep your blood moving through your body. That rhythmic pumping produces the throbbing a person feels during a migraine.

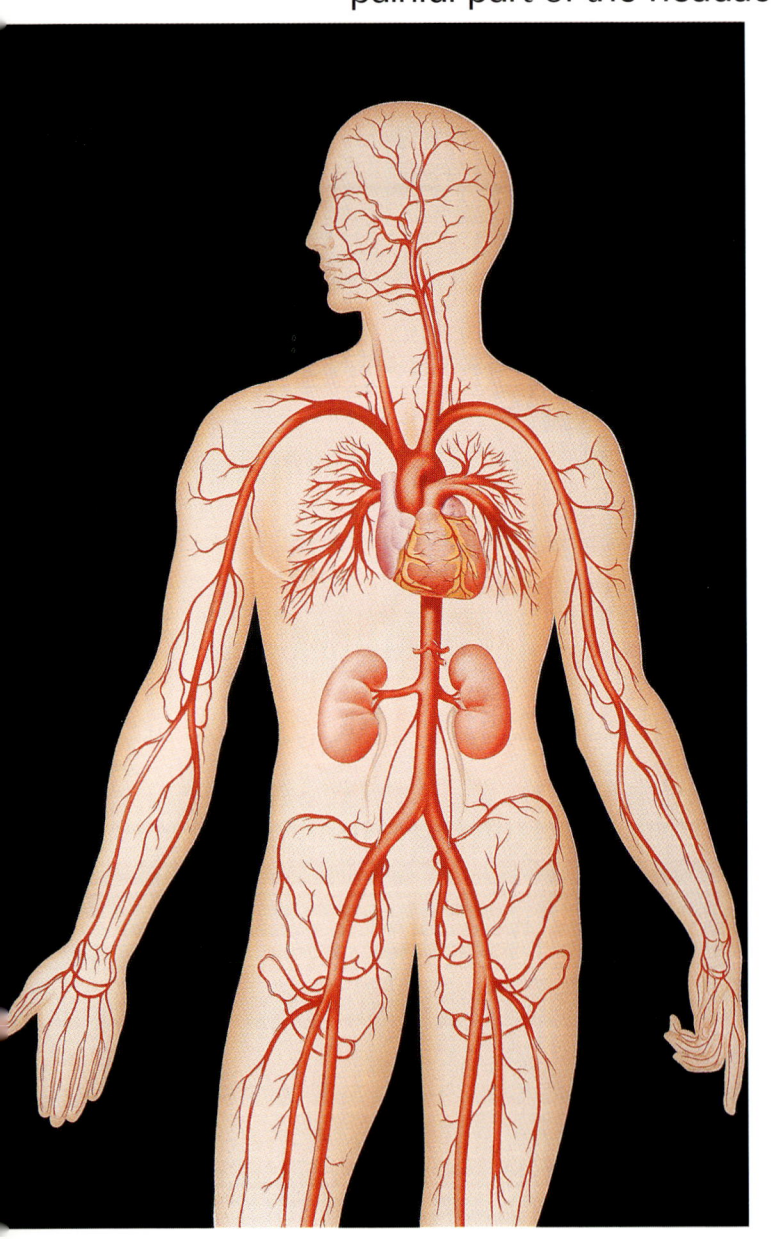

Arteries carry oxygen-rich blood from the heart to all parts of the body.

Activity 1:
The Pulses in Your Head

Has a doctor or nurse ever taken your pulse? He or she was timing your heartbeat by feeling the throbbing beat on the inside of your wrist, where an artery passes close to the surface. You can also feel a person's pulse by pressing against the large blood vessels on the sides of the neck or the forehead.

Try to find all these pulse points on yourself and on a friend. Look at a watch or clock with a second hand and count the number of beats per minute. What is your pulse? Is your friend's higher or lower? Adults normally have a pulse rate of about 70, but a child's pulse beats faster. Exercise and excitement can also make your pulse speed up.

Eventually the swollen blood vessels return to normal, and the migraine eases. Sometimes vomiting or falling asleep helps to end a migraine. After "sleeping it off," a person may wake up feeling refreshed and full of energy. But sometimes feelings of tiredness and listlessness—the migraine "hangover"—drag on for a day or two.

When to See a Doctor

Although millions of people get headaches, doctors don't usually hear about them. Most headaches occur just once in a while and can be relieved by drugs such as aspirin. These headaches do not usually send people rushing to the doctor. But if you get headaches often, or if they make it hard for you to live normally, then it's time to seek medical help.

Aspirin is famous for treating headaches, but it's not a good choice for children.

A doctor may be able to help you figure out what's causing your headaches. Then you can decide what kind of treatment you need. A doctor will also know whether your headaches are a sign of a more serious illness.

First, the doctor will ask you some questions about your headaches. The doctor will want to know when the headaches started, when and how often they occur, how long they last, and which parts of your head hurt. Is the pain dull or sharp, mild or severe, throbbing or constant? Do the headaches start after you eat a certain food, look at a bright light, or when you are physically active? Does the pain get worse when you bend over, cough, sneeze, strain, or move your head suddenly? Do you have problems sleeping?

The doctor will also ask whether you get any warning signs that a headache is coming. Do you experience nausea and vomiting or sensitivity to light, noise, or smells? Have you had any head injuries, serious illnesses, or

Keep a Diary!

It's a good idea to keep a diary of your headaches. Write down the date and time of each headache. Describe what each headache feels like and what you were doing when you got it. These notes can help you remember important details. By looking at a few weeks of your headache records, a doctor may be able to spot a pattern and discover clues to your problem.

surgery for a tumor or a brain disease? Do any of your close relatives have migraines or other headache problems? Your answers to these questions will help the doctor figure out what is causing your headaches.

A complete physical examination can provide additional information. For instance, your headaches may be due to eyestrain. An eye test may show that you need glasses.

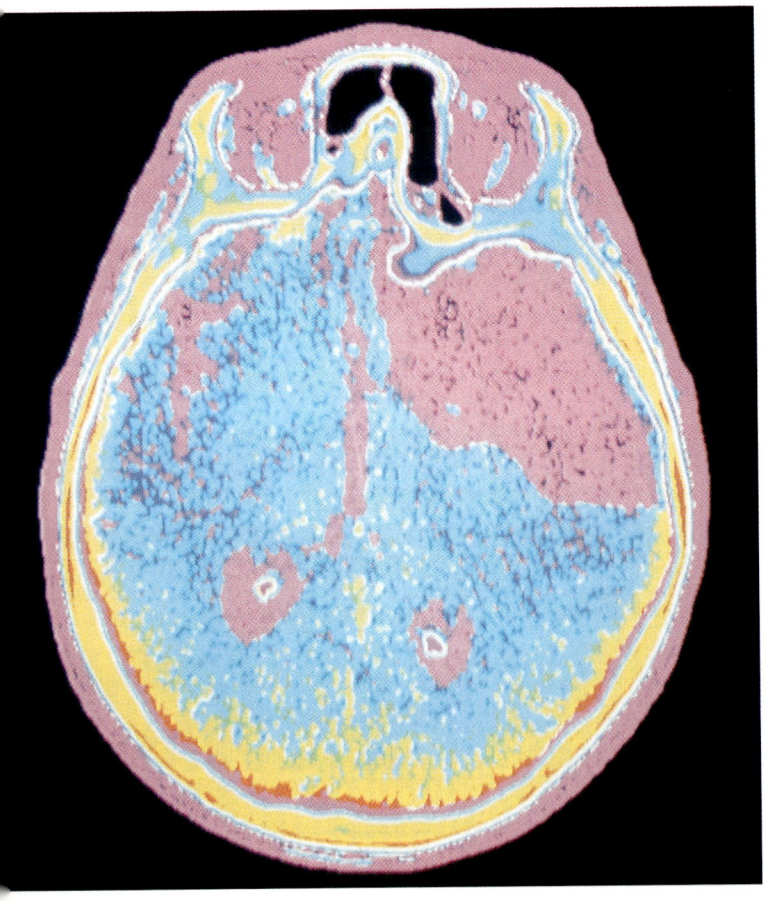

If the doctor thinks the headaches may be signs of a more serious problem, you may be given some other tests. A **CT scan** or **MRI scan** produces revealing pictures of the brain. These tests can show tumors, cysts, abscesses, or other problems. Once the doctor figures out what kind of headaches you've been having, you can start treating them.

This brain scan shows a cyst (pink, right) that may grow larger and cause painful headaches.

Treating Headaches

Many people treat their headaches themselves, without going to a doctor. They take a pain reliever, such as aspirin, acetaminophen (Tylenol), ibuprofen (Advil or Motrin), or naproxen. These drugs are popular because they are usually quick and effective. They are also safe enough to take without a doctor's prescription.

How do pain-relieving drugs work? When body cells or tissues are damaged, they release a chemical called **prostaglandin** (PRAHS-tuh-glandin). This chemical stimulates the nerves that send pain messages to the brain.

Did You Know...

Your brain makes its own painkillers called **endorphins** (en-DOHR-finz). These chemicals attach themselves to nerve cells in the brain and block pain messages.

Aspirin and other pain relievers prevent cells from releasing prostaglandin. When your brain stops getting pain messages, your headache disappears. Aspirin, ibuprofen, and naproxen also help reduce swelling. This decreases the pressure on pain nerves. Some pain medicines, such as Excedrin, contain caffeine. Caffeine helps the pain-relieving drugs work better in the body. It also makes blood vessels constrict, which may help relieve migraine headaches.

Aspirin and Viruses Don't Mix

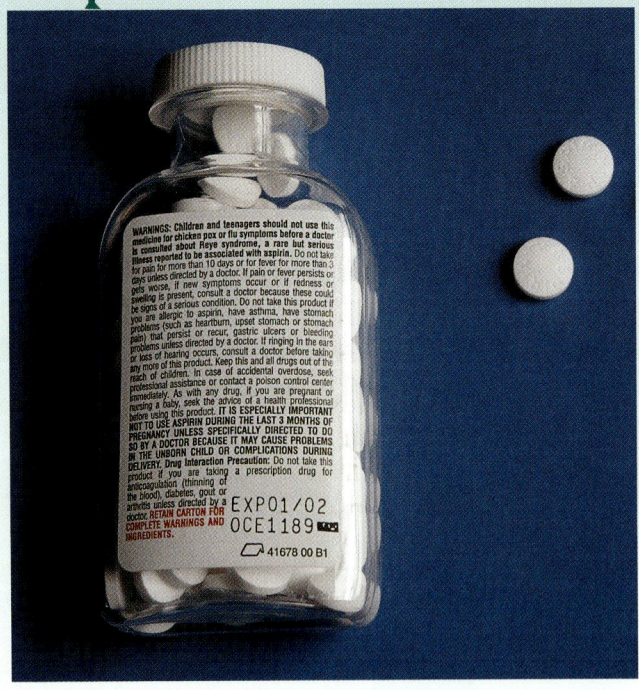

Children should never take aspirin to treat a viral infection such as a cold, the flu, or chickenpox. It can lead to **Reye's syndrome**, a serious and sometimes deadly condition that affects the liver and brain. Many doctors say that kids really shouldn't take aspirin at all. Instead, they should take acetaminophen or ibuprofen.

Children should not take aspirin to treat a cold.

Drugs made from **ergot**—a mold that grows on rye and other grains—were the first medicines used to treat migraines. Chemicals in the mold attach themselves to the same spots on nerve cells as serotonin and make blood vessels constrict. The newest drugs for treating migraines work the same way, but they are much more effective. When these drugs were first developed, they had to be injected into a muscle. Now they are available in pills and in liquids that can be sprayed into the nose.

While you're waiting for a pain reliever to work, you can help a tension-type headache by taking a nap, rubbing your head and neck muscles, putting a hot compress or an ice pack where it hurts, or taking a hot bath. You may be able to ease a migraine headache by lying down in a dark, quiet room. A cold compress or ice pack may help too.

Bed rest and an ice pack are helpful in treating a migraine.

People who get migraines with aura may be able to avoid headache pain if they pay attention to the warning signs. Taking a combination of a pain reliever and caffeine at the first hint of flashing lights or numbness can block the pain messages before they get to the brain.

Headaches may be a sign of stress at school or at home. Your body may respond to these strong feelings by giving you frequent headaches. If this happens, you may want to see a counselor. A counselor can help you get to the root of the problem and deal with it. Eventually, as you overcome your problem, the headaches should lessen or go away completely.

Biofeedback is often an effective way to treat people who get a lot of headaches. In biofeedback, electrodes are

Can this counselor help this girl figure out why she gets so many headaches?

A Neat Trick

During a migraine, extra blood flows into the dilated vessels in the head, so less blood is available to keep the skin of the hands warm. As a result, the person's hands are usually very cold. Biofeedback training can teach a person how to make more blood flow to the hands so that blood vessels in the brain swell less. This can stop migraine pain.

attached to various parts of the body. They track body functions, such as monitor temperature, muscle activity, and heart rate. By watching the tracking instruments while practicing relaxation techniques, a person can learn how to control some of the body's reactions to stress.

People who learn how to relax their muscles can sometimes prevent tension-type headaches before they start. And some people can even stop their migraines by learning how to reduce blood flow to the scalp. This technique prevents arteries in the person's head from throbbing. After practicing with biofeedback electrodes, many people can often stop headaches without using drugs.

Preventing Headaches

There are a number of safe and simple things you can do to lower your risk of getting headaches. If you know what kinds of things give you headaches, try to stay away from them. For instance, if you notice that you get headaches after eating bacon or hot dogs, don't eat those foods.

Stay away from foods that may give you a headache. Eating the right foods will keep your body healthy.

35

You can also avoid getting headaches by sticking to a daily routine. A healthy body needs a good night's sleep and enough energy to keep it going all day. So get to bed on time and don't skip meals or wait too long to eat.

You may get a headache when you watch TV or play computer games for a long time. If this happens, take frequent breaks. Just gaze into space and chill out, or get up and move around.

Stress is not always easy to avoid, but you can learn how to relieve it. Taking slow, deep breaths can help release tension. This can prevent your muscles from tightening, and may keep a tension-type headache from starting. Meditation also helps lower the heart rate and blood pressure and reduces stress. Using your imagination to create a soothing picture in your mind can help you relax too.

Taking frequent breaks can keep your eyes from getting overworked.

When you run and jump and get plenty of regular exercise, your brain makes extra endorphins. These natural chemicals can help you avoid headaches. You can also do exercises to relax the muscles in your neck, shoulders, jaw, and back. You may not be able to completely avoid getting headaches, but following these good health practices will make them much less likely to happen.

Regular exercise produces extra endorphins, which can help stop headaches before they start.

Activity 2:
How Common Are Headaches?

You can find out just how common headaches are by taking a survey of your friends and relatives. What kind of headaches do they get? Compare the number of people who get tension-type headaches to the number who get migraines. Try to include people of different ages and both sexes. Ask each one the following questions:

Have you ever had a headache? If so, how often?

What do your headaches feel like? Do you get the dull, constant pain of a tension-type headache or the painful throbbing of a migraine? Where is the pain? Do you get different kinds of headaches?

Do you know what kinds of things cause your headaches? How do you ease the pain of a headache? Do pain relievers help, or do you need to go to the doctor?

Look over the results carefully. Do you find that adults get more headaches than children? Do they occur more in one sex than the other? What other interesting things have you discovered?

Glssary

artery—one of the large blood vessels that carries blood from the heart to the rest of the body

aura—a warning period shortly before a migraine headache. Warning signs include flashing lights, bright, zigzag lines, blind spots, numbness or a feeling of pins and needles in the lips or hands.

biofeedback—a method of learning how to control certain body processes, including temperature, blood pressure, and muscle tension

blood vessel—one of the tubes that carries blood throughout the body

caffeine—a chemical that stimulates the body and causes blood vessels to constrict

constrict—to become narrow

CT scan—also CAT (computerized axial tomography) scan, a test in which X rays are sent through the body at various angles to examine soft tissues

dilate—to widen

endorphin—a chemical in the body that acts as a natural painkiller

ergot—the first drug used to treat migraines

hallucination—a mental state in which a person sees and hears things that are not there

migraine—a severe, throbbing headache that occurs when blood vessels to the brain become narrow and then widen. Other symptoms such as nausea and vomiting often accompany the headache.

MRI scan—a picture of body tissues created by an imaging technique called magnetic resonance imaging

nerve—a structure that carries messages to and from the brain

prodrome—a warning period up to 24 hours before a migraine headache begins; warning signs may include depression, irritability, restlessness, mood swings, speech or memory problems, a loss of appetite, or a sensitivity to lights, sounds, and smells.

prostaglandin—a chemical in the body that stimulates nerve endings that send pain messages to the brain

Reye's syndrome—a rare but serious illness that is associated with taking aspirin during a viral infection

scalp—the skin on the top of your head. It is usually covered with hair.

serotonin—a chemical in the brain that controls a person's mood, sleep habits, and the narrowing and widening of blood vessels

tension-type headache—a dull, constant pain caused when muscles in the face, neck, and scalp tighten for a long period of time

tumor—a cluster of rapidly growing cells. Some tumors cause cancer.

Learning More

Books

Bic, Zuzana and L. Francis Bic. *No More Headaches, No More Migraines*. Garden City Park, NY: Avery, 1999.

Elkind, Arthur. *Migraines: Everything You Need to Know About Their Cause and Cure*. New York: Avon, 1997.

Garcia-Mendez, Leonardo. *Headaches in Children*. Columbia, Missouri: Lemar, 1996.

Robbins, Lawrence and Susan S. Lang. *Headache Help*. Boston: Houghton Mifflin, 2000.

Organizations and Online Sites

American Council for Headache Education (ACHE)
19 Mantua Road
Mt. Royal, NJ 08061
http://www.achenet.org

Chronic Headaches in Kids
http://ww.mayohealth.org/mayo/9903/htm/chronich.htm
This site has lots of useful information about headaches.

National Headache Foundation
428 W. Saint James Place, 2nd Floor
Chicago, IL 60614-2750
http://www.headaches.org
This National Headache Foundation web site contains sections designed especially for kids, for their parents, and for school health professionals.

Oooh, Your Aching Head!
http://kidshealth.org/kid/normal/headache.html
This site has easy-to-read information about headaches. It is perfect for curious kids.

When Kids Get Headaches
http://kidshealth.org/parent/general/aches/headache.html
More kid-friendly information about headaches.

Index

Page numbers in *italics* indicate illustrations.

About the Authors

Dr. Alvin Silverstein is a professor of biology at the College of Staten Island of the City University of New York. **Virginia B. Silverstein** is a translator of Russian scientific literature. The Silversteins first worked together on a research project at the University of Pennsylvania. Since then, they have produced 6 children and more than 160 published books for young people.

Laura Silverstein Nunn, a graduate of Kean College, has been helping with her parents' books since her high school days. She is the coauthor of more than thirty books on diseases and health, science concepts, endangered species, and pets. Laura lives with her husband Matt and their young son Cory in a rural New Jersey town not far from her childhood home.